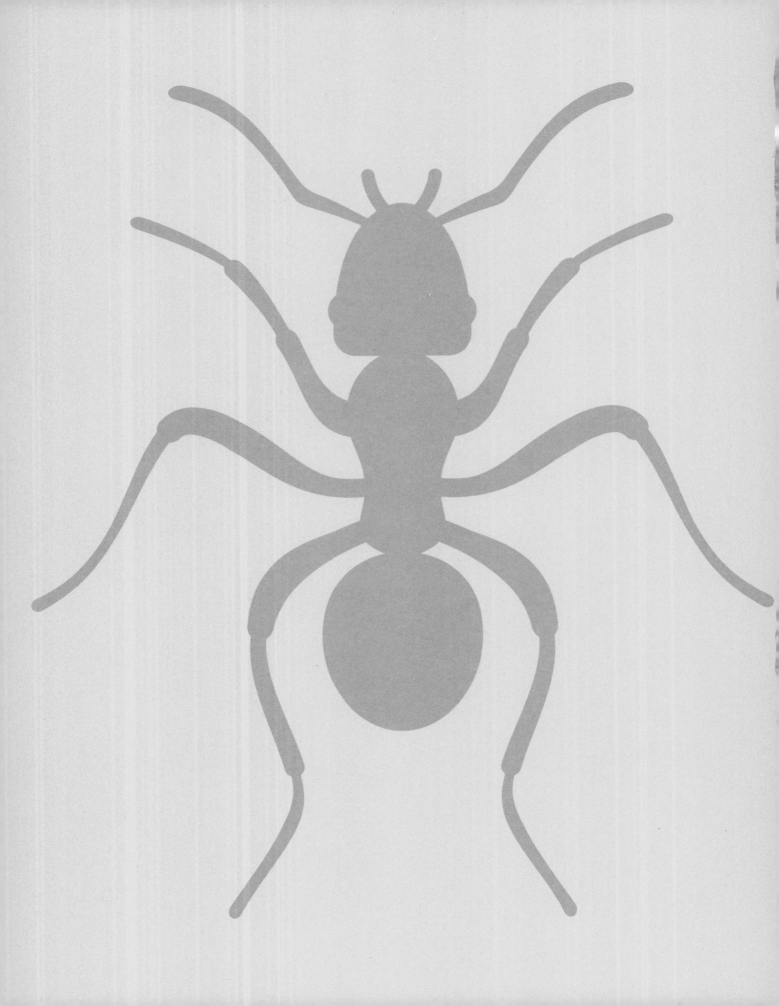

BUGS

Big & Small
God Made Them All

Will Zinke

First printing: September 2014
Third printing: June 2020

Master Books®, P.O. Box 726, Green Forest, AR 72638

Master Books® is a division of the New Leaf Publishing Group, Inc.

ISBN: 978-0-89051-835-9
ISBN: 978-1-61458-412-4 (digital)

Library of Congress Number: 2014941497

Cover & Interior Design: Diana Bogardus

Unless otherwise noted, Scripture quotations are from the New King James Version of the Bible.

Please consider requesting that a copy of this volume be purchased by your local library system.

Printed in China

Please visit our website for other great titles: www.masterbooks.com

For information regarding author interviews, please contact the publicity department at (870) 438-5288.

Master Books®
A Division of New Leaf Publishing Group
www.masterbooks.com

About the author:

Will Zinke has been fascinated with the insect world ever since he saw a goliath beetle in a museum at the age of seven. He holds a BS in biology and has taught science for over ten years. He was home schooled and is now home schooling his four children. He is currently assisting Dr. Gary Parker with the Creation Adventures Museum in Florida, conducting fossil and insect adventures with his wife, Amy, and their children.

Photo credits:

All bugs are insects,
but not all insects are bugs!

AMAZING Creepy Crawlers

BUGS! They are everywhere! Those amazing creepy crawlers all have special and sometimes incredible jobs that their Creator gave them to do. With so many bugs on planet Earth, God must think they are pretty important!

What are bugs? Well, let's set the record straight: "All bugs are insects, but not all insects are bugs," or so the saying goes. This means that the term "bug" refers to just one order of insects. Generally, there are over 40 insect orders. Some examples are the beetles (*Coleoptera*, meaning "sheath wing"), the butterflies and moths (*Lepidoptera*, which means "scale wing"), and the flies (order *Diptera*, or "two wing").

Insects, with their three body parts and six legs, are small signposts pointing to God's infinite creativity. With their alluring beauty, incredible design features, and limitless variety, they are a testament to our all-wise and wonderful Creator! In this book we will show you just a few of the most amazing, strange, and wonderful examples of insects that God has made!

So why did God make insects? Well, without insects such as bees, butterflies, hornets, and beetles, many plants would not be able to reproduce. Pollination, anyone? And without insects such as flies, ants, and dung beetles, the world would be a very smelly place, because they are scavengers and decomposers. God made insects to keep things running smoothly. Let's take a look at how important just one insect, the honey bee, is!

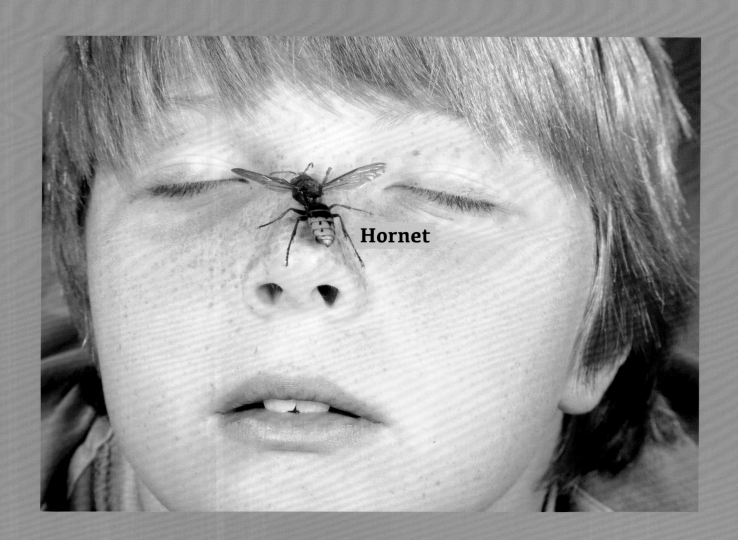

Hornet

When you think of a bee, you may think of enjoying their honey or the fear of being stung in your garden. Bees are so important to the environment because of being a pollinator. Pollinators are insects and other creatures that transfer pollen or seeds from one flower to another, fertilizing them so they can grow to produce many foods we like to eat and flowers we enjoy just looking at, like roses.

The honey bee seems to be disappearing and that has alarmed both farmers and scientists. In the past few years, bee colonies have been discovered that appear to be abandoned and have vanished without a trace, something called "colony collapse disorder." Many studies have taken place to try to solve this mystery that threatens part of the ecosystem.

Pesticides, chemicals used to kill bugs and weeds, are one cause that many blame for this decline in honey bee populations. Other studies have focused on fewer and less diverse food sources because of a decline in the variety of crops taking up the space in gardens and farms, leaving no room for other plants that may have longer flowering times.

Often a bee eats from a specific type of flower as long as it is available, making sure the right pollen gets to the right flowers.

creepy cool!

Pollination

Some plants can pollinate themselves without help, but many cannot, so they need something to do it for them. Bees are helpful pollinators, and the process normally goes like this:

1 Bees are attracted to flowers to consume nectar and pollen.

2 Pollen is collected on the bee's body while it is feeding.

3 The bee carries the pollen to another plant, leaving pollen, and fertilizing the flower.

Without bees we wouldn't have cherries, blueberries, apples, onions, cucumbers, avacados, oranges, or Brazil nuts!

creepy cool!

But what if the bee is missing and cannot pollinate the flowers?

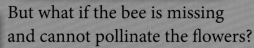

3 Blossoms appear on an apple tree, but no bees are available to pollinate.

2 The blossoms do not develop into fruit.

1 No fruit to eat!

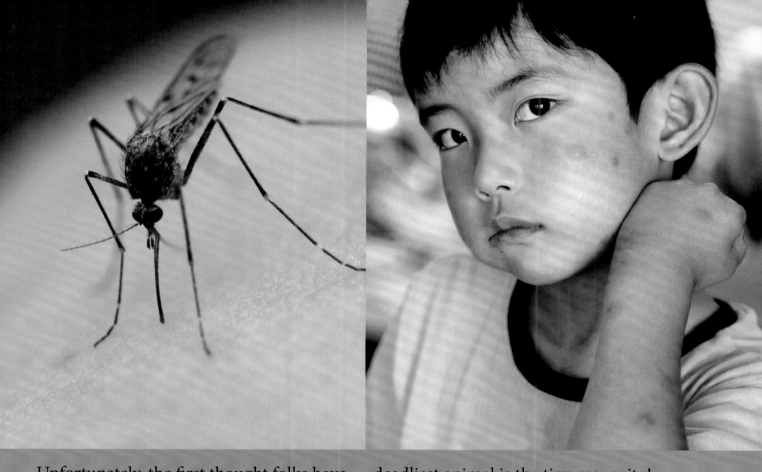

Unfortunately, the first thought folks have when they hear the word bug is, "Yuck! Quick, get the bug spray!" It is true that the common insects that live close to us are usually pests that bring disease, such as roaches, mosquitoes, and fleas. In fact, do you know what the most deadly animal on earth is today? Not the lion. Not the cobra. Not even the great white shark. The deadliest animal is the tiny mosquito! Thousands of people die every day from diseases transmitted by mosquitoes. But did you know that the male mosquito is a vegetarian, only eating sap and plant juices? In fact, not all species are blood-suckers, and even the blood-loving females also eat plant juices and only use blood as a supplement for their eggs.

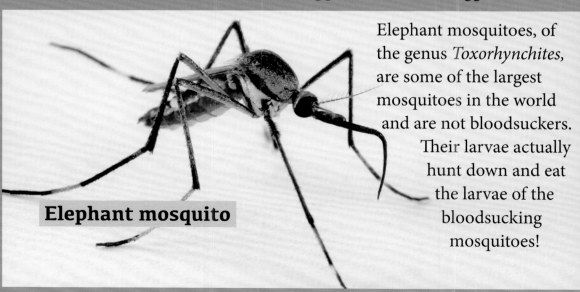

Elephant mosquito

Elephant mosquitoes, of the genus *Toxorhynchites*, are some of the largest mosquitoes in the world and are not bloodsuckers. Their larvae actually hunt down and eat the larvae of the bloodsucking mosquitoes!

Another question might be, "Why would God make these awful bugs?" Well, we know that the Bible says that everything God created was "very good" in the beginning; it was man's sin that brought corruption and death upon the whole creation. It was probably at this time that some creatures that once ate only plants and provided good benefits became carnivores and parasites. Where once life was easy and safe, now it would be dreadfully difficult. As we read in Genesis 3:18, *"Both thorns and thistles it shall bring forth for you. . . ."* Their lives no longer a picnic in the park, our first parents (Adam and Eve) were beginning to see the terrible price of their sin as everything around them changed.

Treehoppers

But we have hope! In Genesis 3:15 our Savior is first mentioned, a deliverer who would someday set things right again! One who would "crush" the head of the serpent (Satan). And we have this hope not because we are developing better cures for diseases or using our own intellect to save the planet, but because of the shed blood of Jesus, our Redeemer, who has promised to return again! In Romans 8:21–22 we read: *"…because the creation itself also will be delivered from the bondage of corruption into the glorious liberty of the children of God. For we know that the whole creation groans and labors with birth pangs together until now."* Oh, what a wonderful day it will be when Christ returns!

Let's take a look at some of the most amazing creatures found all over the Earth!

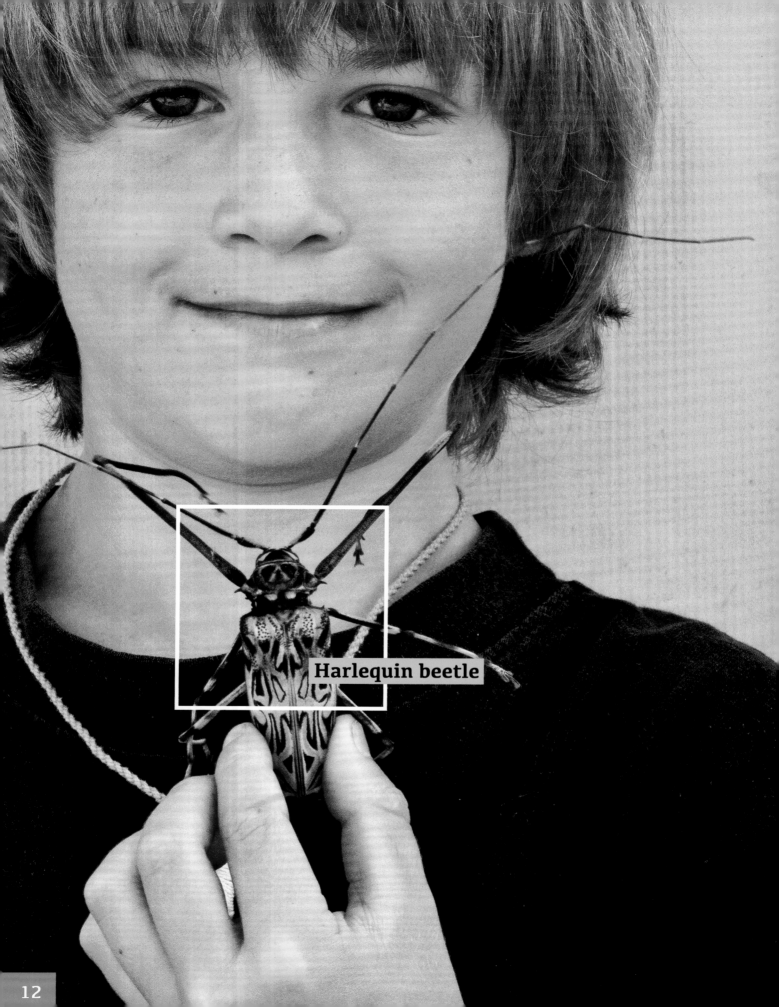

Harlequin beetle

JUMBO GIANTS

There are way more insects than any other animal on planet Earth. In fact, there are so many insects that if we had a really big scale large enough to place all the world's elephants on one side and all the world's insects on the other, guess which would be heavier? That's right, the insects! There are so many bugs, with new ones being discovered each year. Maybe someday you will find a new one! For now, let's look at some of the biggest!

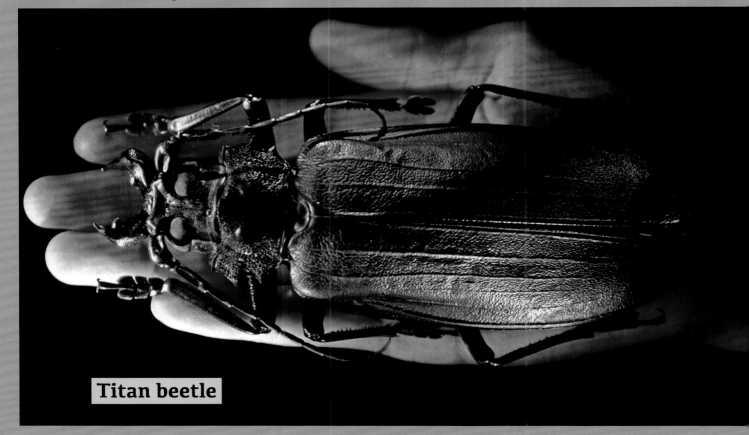

Titan beetle

One of the world's largest beetles, with lengths up to seven inches (over 17 cm), these living tanks are also considered the strongest creatures for their size! An adult **Hercules beetle** (*Dynastes hercules*) can lift or pull objects many times its own weight. If we had that strength, lifting a car over our head would be no problem! Their strength comes from the thick muscle strands (ligaments) connecting their legs to the rest of their hard exoskeleton.

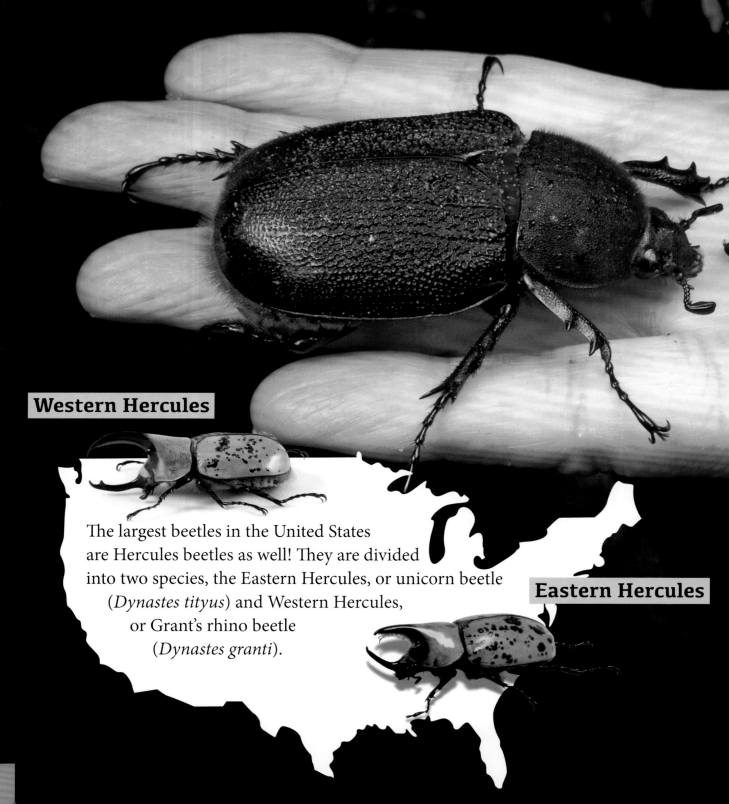

Western Hercules

Eastern Hercules

The largest beetles in the United States are Hercules beetles as well! They are divided into two species, the Eastern Hercules, or unicorn beetle (*Dynastes tityus*) and Western Hercules, or Grant's rhino beetle (*Dynastes granti*).

The incredible variety in horn structure points to a wonderfully imaginative Creator who designs form with beauty and function! The males use their immense horns in battles over food, sometimes for a mate, and in balancing and steering during flight. Yes, these guys actually fly!

Megasoma grub

Elephant
beetle

Elephant beetles (*Megasoma*) are also considered among the largest and heaviest of all insects. They get their name from their bulky size and long trunk-like horn. **Megasoma acteon** and **Megasoma elephas** can be over five inches (12.7 cm) long! It is quite an amazing feat of engineering that allows these huge creatures to fly. Just think what is required to lift such a heavy insect and keep it in flight. Children of the Amazon rainforest often collect these large beetles as pets!

Their larvae, or grubs, can be as large as a man's hand! Like butterflies, beetles go through complete metamorphosis, with a caterpillar-like larval stage, a pupa stage, and finally an adult flying stage that is completely different from the larva. Most giant beetles spend their larval stage consuming rotting logs or other decaying plant material. They are a very important part of the decomposition process in tropical forests. *Megasoma* grubs can reach a weight of almost half a pound, and they are also a tasty part of many people's diet in the rainforest! Yummy!

get some grub?

Entomophagy is a big word given for those who eat insects for food, from Australia to Africa to Asia to the United States!

creepy cool!

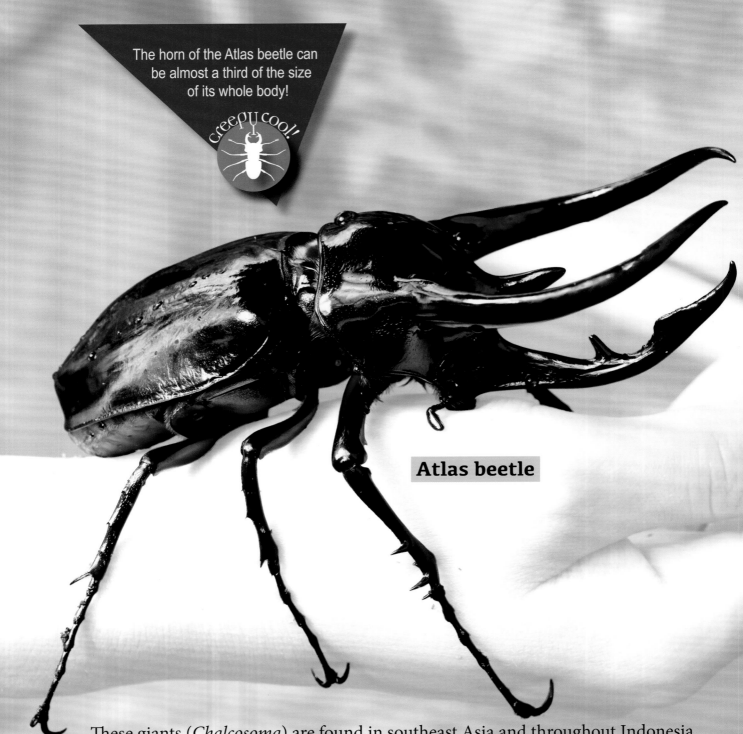

The horn of the Atlas beetle can be almost a third of the size of its whole body!

creepy cool!

Atlas beetle

These giants (*Chalcosoma*) are found in southeast Asia and throughout Indonesia. They are another one of the world's largest beetles with lengths reaching over five inches (12.7 cm)! The Psalmist said, *"O LORD, how manifold are Your works! In wisdom You have made them all. The earth is full of Your possessions" (Psalm 104:24).* These amazing insects are a testimony to their Creator!

Notice the horn design on the Atlas beetle. Does it remind you of a certain dinosaur? Perhaps Triceratops? Some evolutionists claim that similar designs found in animals throughout nature are due to things changing in similar ways over time. The creation model assumes that common design features point to a common Designer, rather than a common ancestor!

Named after the giant that David fought in the Bible, these beetles are truly huge! **Goliath beetles** live in Sub-Saharan Africa and are in the "flower beetle" family, just like the North American "June bug." They may not be as long as the Hercules or elephant beetle, but they rival them in their weight. There are several types that thrive in the humid tropical forests of West Equatorial Africa, all the way to the drier savannahs of East Africa. Collectors prize them for their size and color variations.

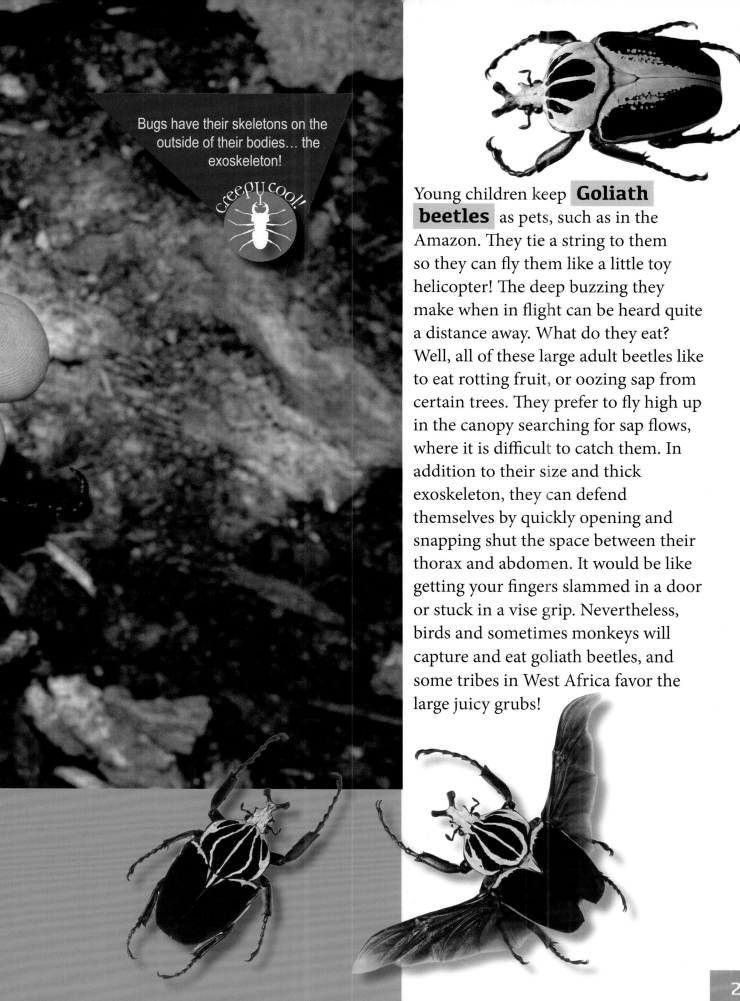

Young children keep **Goliath beetles** as pets, such as in the Amazon. They tie a string to them so they can fly them like a little toy helicopter! The deep buzzing they make when in flight can be heard quite a distance away. What do they eat? Well, all of these large adult beetles like to eat rotting fruit, or oozing sap from certain trees. They prefer to fly high up in the canopy searching for sap flows, where it is difficult to catch them. In addition to their size and thick exoskeleton, they can defend themselves by quickly opening and snapping shut the space between their thorax and abdomen. It would be like getting your fingers slammed in a door or stuck in a vise grip. Nevertheless, birds and sometimes monkeys will capture and eat goliath beetles, and some tribes in West Africa favor the large juicy grubs!

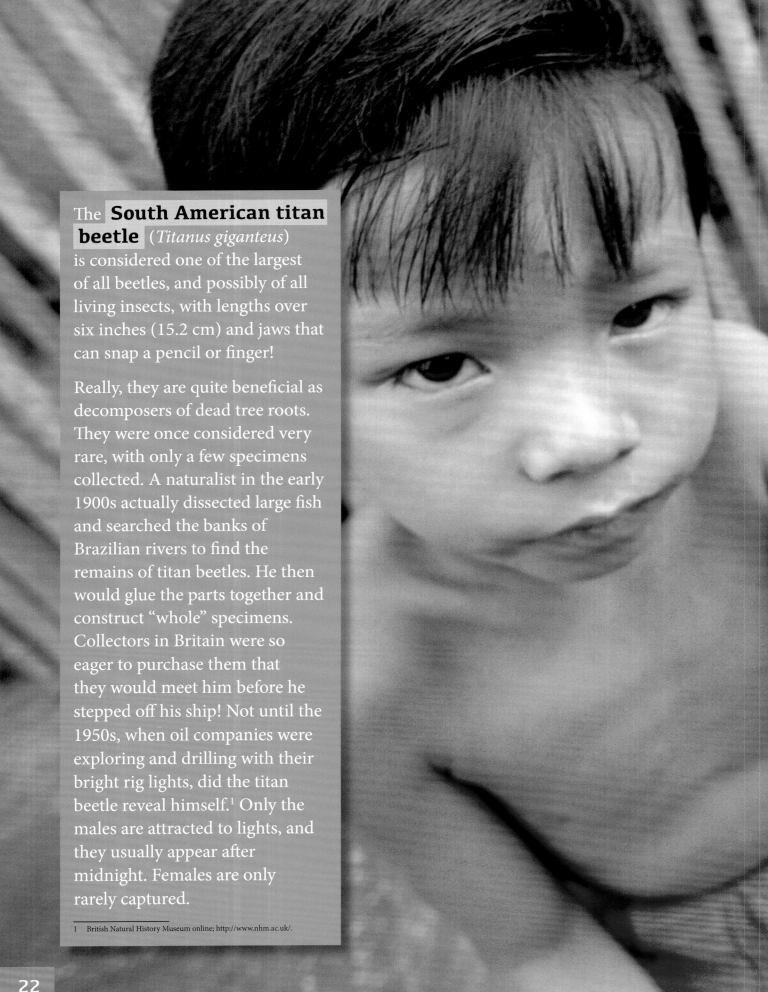

The **South American titan beetle** (*Titanus giganteus*) is considered one of the largest of all beetles, and possibly of all living insects, with lengths over six inches (15.2 cm) and jaws that can snap a pencil or finger!

Really, they are quite beneficial as decomposers of dead tree roots. They were once considered very rare, with only a few specimens collected. A naturalist in the early 1900s actually dissected large fish and searched the banks of Brazilian rivers to find the remains of titan beetles. He then would glue the parts together and construct "whole" specimens. Collectors in Britain were so eager to purchase them that they would meet him before he stepped off his ship! Not until the 1950s, when oil companies were exploring and drilling with their bright rig lights, did the titan beetle reveal himself.[1] Only the males are attracted to lights, and they usually appear after midnight. Females are only rarely captured.

1   British Natural History Museum online; http://www.nhm.ac.uk/.

Titan beetle

Here is the largest beetle next to the smallest beetle, a "feather winged" beetle (*Ptiliidae* family) just 0.2 inches (.5 cm)… so small they do not use wings but tiny thread-like appendages to fly! Titan beetles are members of the "longhorn" family of beetles, which includes other giant beetles.

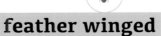

actual size

close up

feather winged

Titan beetle

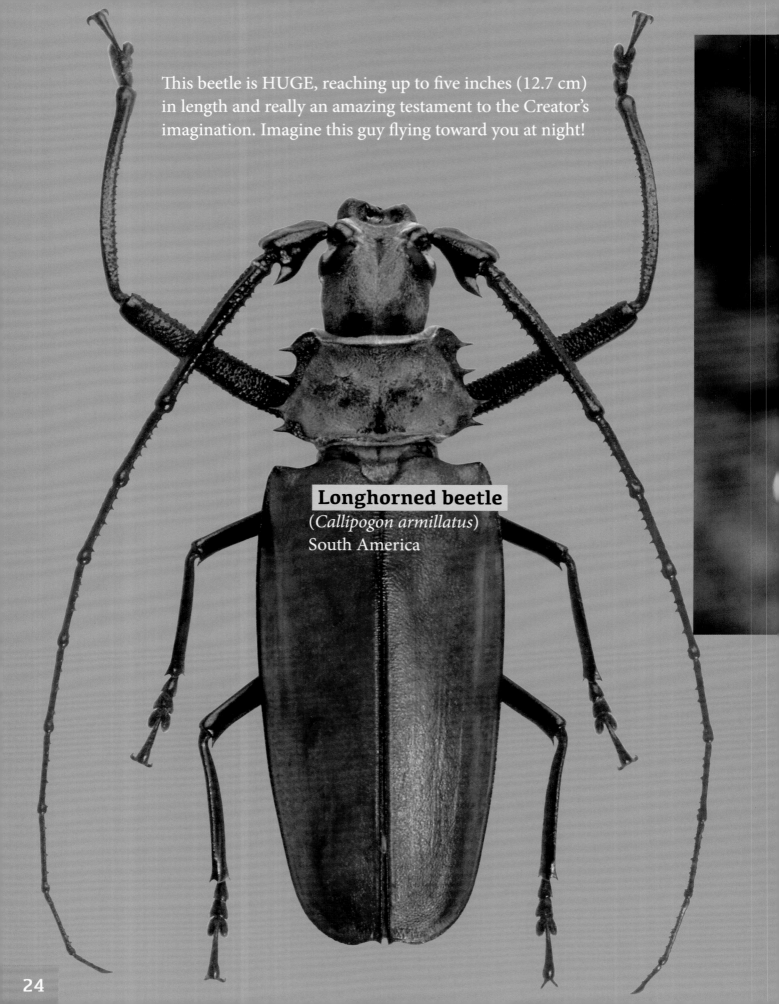

This beetle is HUGE, reaching up to five inches (12.7 cm) in length and really an amazing testament to the Creator's imagination. Imagine this guy flying toward you at night!

Longhorned beetle
(*Callipogon armillatus*)
South America

The Large toothed longhorn beetle spends up to ten years of its life in the larva stage!

creepy cool!

Here is the **Large toothed longhorn beetle** (*Macrodontia cervicornis*) of South America.

These beetles are beautifully patterned yet have HUGE jaws called "mandibles" that can give a painful pinch! This interesting beetle has a clever pattern on its wing covers to help it hide among the fallen leaves of the forest. They are not predators but, surprisingly, just suck on tree sap. The larvae of this beetle feed on decaying wood and have been considered a delicacy for hundreds of years. These beetles are considered one of the largest species in the world, with lengths reaching seven inches (17.8 cm)!

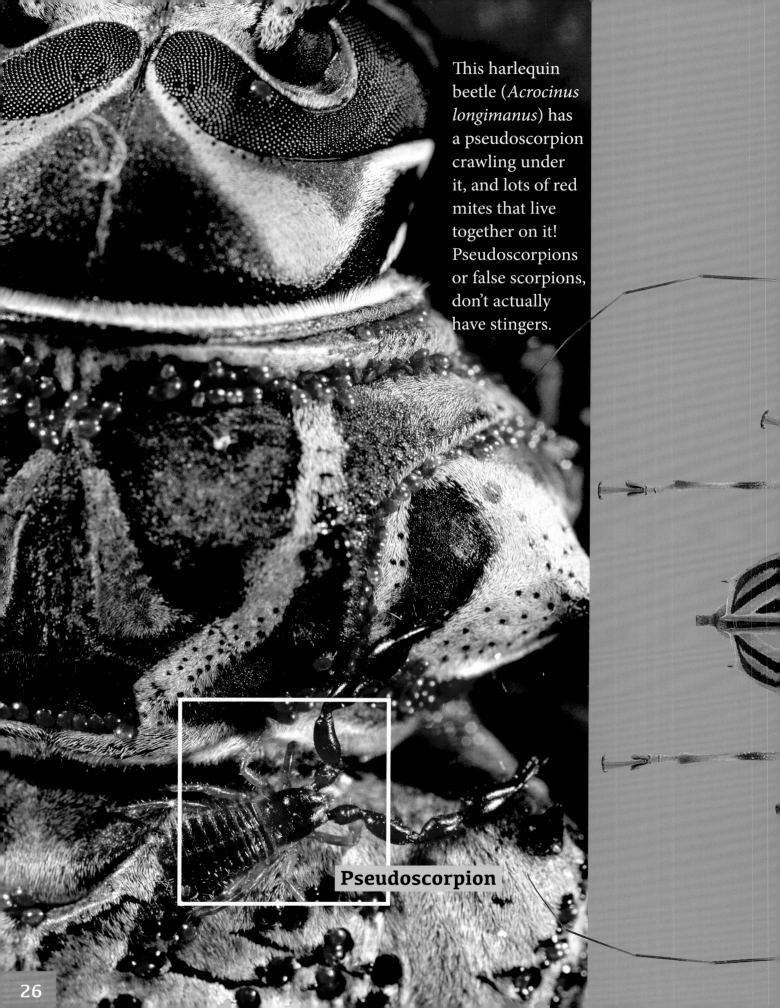

This harlequin beetle (*Acrocinus longimanus*) has a pseudoscorpion crawling under it, and lots of red mites that live together on it! Pseudoscorpions or false scorpions, don't actually have stingers.

Pseudoscorpion

Check out the five-inch (12.7 cm) spread on those arms! The South American **Harlequin beetle** has extended front legs in the male, used in mating displays for a female that are similar to the horns of a rhino beetle or jaws of a stag beetle. Some say that the amazing colors and patterns on this incredible beetle gives inspiration for the shields used by local inhabitants! In 2003, researchers discovered an amazing antifungal property in this beetle that is being further studied to help fight resistant strains of fungal infections in people.

Another interesting family is the weevil (*Curculionidae*). They come in all shapes and sizes, and this family is considered to be one of the largest in the animal kingdom! In some parts of the world, their grubs are considered a delicacy. Pictured is the largest weevil in the world, **Macrochirus praetor** of Malaysia.

photo credit Audubon Nature Institute.

Flower beetle

Similar to their fancy fluttering friend, the butterflies, these beetles like to visit flowers, fruits, and flowing sap from trees. Appropriately named "flower beetles" or "fruit chaffers" (*Chelorrina polyphemus* of Central Africa), they are also very important as pollinators, and their larvae help decompose fallen logs and other plant matter. Their amazing array of colors and patterns, given by God, make them a favorite group of insects to collect and study!

Jamaican giant swallowtails

of Jamaica are the largest butterflies of the western hemisphere!

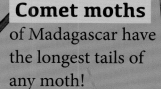

Comet moths

of Madagascar have the longest tails of any moth!

Birdwings

of New Guinea are some of the largest butterflies in the world with a wingspan of almost 11 inches (28 cm)!

Jungle nymphs

of Malaysia lay the largest eggs of any insect!

White witch moths

of South and Central America have the largest wingspan of any moth– over 11 inches!

Atlas moths

of Southeast Asia and Indonesia have wingspans over 10 inches!

Giant wetas

of New Zealand are like oversized crickets!

Termite mound

Weird & wonderful

Insects have enthralled people for thousands of years. They have been used as color for our clothes (cochineal and carmine-red dye from the scale insect *Dactylopius coccus*), jewelry for beauty (*buprestid* and *cetonid* beetles), and even as food (weevil and other large beetle grubs as well as termites)! In East Africa, great swarms of winged termites leave the mounds on the first heavy rain after the dry season. Children will tap the nests with sticks to trick the insects into thinking the rain has started. When the winged adults emerge, the children quickly grab them, popping them into their mouth. They say they are *tamu sana* or "very sweet"! And who could forget that special diet of John the Baptist — locusts and honey. And with that said, here are some more weird and wonderful insects!

Termite swarm

Namib Desert beetles, also called the Fog basking beetle (*Stenocara*), have a wonderful design to get moisture from one of the driest environments on Earth. During sunrise in the Namib Desert of southwest Africa, a light fog sometimes drifts over the sand dunes. The Creator has given these little beetles a very bumpy shell on their backs, which when examined was shown to attract and collect water directly from the air! The low valleys and grooves of the shell actually repel water. As these beetles do a "headstand" it allows the tiny moisture droplets to flow down the small grooves to form large drops of water, right to the beetle's mouth!

Namib Desert beetle

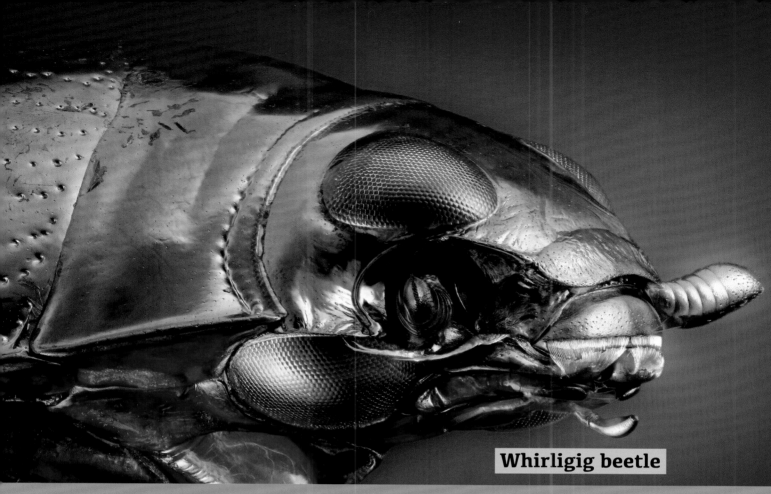

Whirligig beetle

You may be familiar with these common little spinning beetles found in the calm areas of streams and lakes. Looking like a swarm of flies zigzagging across the surface of the water, they can sometimes be a bit intimidating! But these guys have been designed with an incredible set of four eyes that can see underwater as well as above at the same time. They have special binocular vision to help them catch other little insects that they eat. Amazing! And they fly as well!

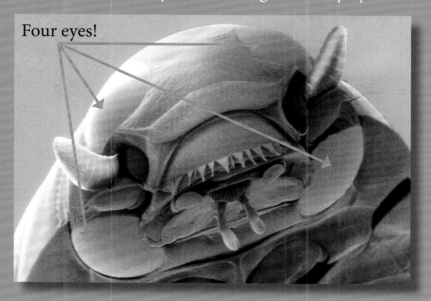

Four eyes!

Predaceous diving beetle

Here is the original air, sea, and land vehicle! Diving beetles can submerge themselves for at least ten minutes by utilizing their specially designed wing covers (elytra) and hairs (setae) on their abdomens to trap a bubble of air. Designed like a streamlined submarine, these beetles can scoot along a river bottom with their paddled back legs searching for their next meal. At night, they take to the air to locate a mate. Diving beetles are a common find under bright lights during warm summer evenings. But beware, they produce an awful-smelling chemical that is said to help them glide effortlessly under water!

Mole beetle

The mole beetle (*Hypocephalus armatus*) is a very unusual insect with specially designed legs for burrowing! This rare beetle is found in a very small area of Brazil, and is only seen above ground during the December rains. It is wingless and cannot fly, and in fact, its wing covers are fused shut.

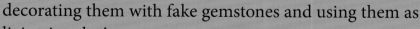

The beautiful **Ironclad beetle** (*Zopherus nodulosus haldemani*) is found in arid regions of northern Mexico and Texas and has an amazingly tough exoskeleton that helps hold water and protect it from predators. The shell is so hard that pinning a specimen is nearly impossible; a small drill bit is recommended! These beetles cannot fly, as their elytra are fused together, and they only eat lichen from the bark of certain trees. They are masters at playing possum, and can keep still for long periods of time until danger is averted. Some children enjoy decorating them with fake gemstones and using them as living jewelry!

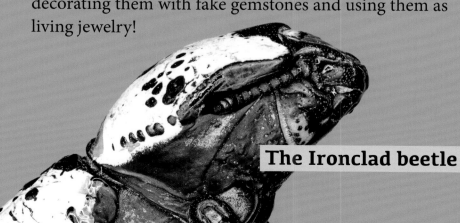

The Ironclad beetle

Coprophanaeus lancifer

Here are God's "clean-up crew"! Dung beetles have long been famous for the way they roll droppings away and bury them for their larvae to feast upon (it is the "juice" formed in the animal's intestines that they crave!). Many of the members of this species stay with their mates and dig tunnels under the dung and help each other in the protection and rearing of young. There are actually three kinds of dung beetles — rollers (which form a ball and roll it away), tunnellers (which tunnel directly below the dung pile and are usually more family-minded), and dwellers (which live directly in the dung pile). All three kinds may be present to help recycle that yummy, delicious dung! It has been said that a typical cow patty can be dispersed in about 24 hours, and in Africa, one pile of elephant dung could house thousands of dung beetles!

Dung beetles

Yes, that's POOP!

In Australia, many species of dung beetle have been successfully imported to assist in cleaning up the countryside from all those sheep and cattle. The world's largest dung beetles (*Heliocopris*) are found in Africa and Southeast Asia, and of course they specialize in elephant droppings! One of the largest dung beetles in South America is a beautiful purple color and cleans up carrion and decaying fungus. Recent research has shown that dung beetles actually navigate using polarized light from the sun and moon …and even more interesting, they are the first creature proven to use star light to keep their dung rolling in a straight line. Their immune system is also being studied to perhaps open up new discoveries that will help us fight diseases!

Rainbow dung beetle

Giraffe weevils (*Trachelophorus giraffe*) are awesome little guys with enlarged heads that extend over half of their body length! Only about an inch long, they are found in the tropical forests of Madagascar. The males use their long necks in mating rituals, and the females use their smaller necks to roll leaves to make their nests.

The female weevil lays just one egg on a leaf, then proceeds to roll it up to keep it safe and provide food when it hatches!

creepy cool!

These true bugs from Thailand and Indonesia really do appear to have a human face! What an amazing design from our loving Creator! (See more about true bugs on page 48!)

Man face bugs
(*Catacanthus incarnatus*)

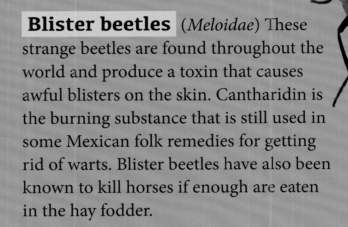

Blister beetles (*Meloidae*) These strange beetles are found throughout the world and produce a toxin that causes awful blisters on the skin. Cantharidin is the burning substance that is still used in some Mexican folk remedies for getting rid of warts. Blister beetles have also been known to kill horses if enough are eaten in the hay fodder.

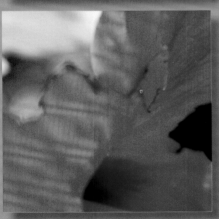

8 out of every 10 animals on Earth are insects!

creepy cool!

Bombardier beetles
(*Brachinus*)

"Ready, aim, fire!" God has given these little guys a set of "cannons" that deliver chemical explosions of searing 212-degree heat to scare away potential predators. The amazing design consists of special glands and chambers that produce and hold volatile chemicals and a turret system that directs the gaseous explosion in whatever direction needed!

This bug is actually just a look-alike of the bombardier beetle, and is in the leaf beetle family, not the ground beetle family. Can you see major differences in the coloring? Bombardier beetles have a dark underbody, while this mimic beetle is bright orange underneath. Learn to look at every detail!

Psalm 139:14 says, *"I will praise You, for I am fearfully and wonderfully made; Marvelous are Your works, And that my soul knows very well."* If God cared enough to design this little creature with these amazing cannons to protect itself, how much more does He care for you, the crown of His creation?

God's amazing night lights
(*Lampyridae*)

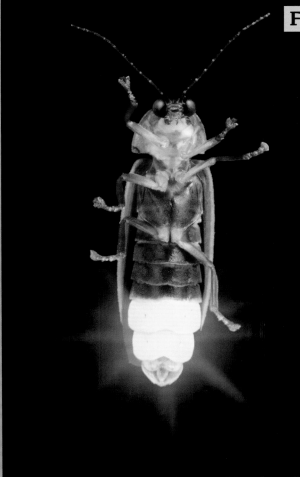

Fireflies

How many of us have fond memories of catching "fireflies" on warm summer nights? Here is another shining example of God's design in His small creations! With over 2,000 known types, fireflies use a complex arrangement of chemicals to produce bright, visible light. Called *bioluminescence,* it is also found in certain deep-sea creatures. Fireflies use luciferin and the enzyme luciferase in combination with oxygen, magnesium, and ATP to produce cold light. They glow from their abdomen, and their larvae are called "glow worms." Some species are so bright, you need to catch just a few to read a book! Some tropical species "blink in sync" and light up the forest with their choreographed light show!

Luciferin and luciferase are named after the deceiver and "angel of light," Lucifer.

creepy cool!

Click beetles
(*Elateridae*)

Have you ever caught a click beetle, laid it on its back, and then watched it "click" and shoot straight up in the air? Equipped with a special hinge system between the thorax and abdomen, these guys can propel themselves up, up, and away and hopefully land back on their feet. They have a special prong and groove designed into their underside that gives them that special bounce! Some are beautiful and large, but most are small and dull-colored. Some species, called "eyed elaters," have large, dark eyespots on their thorax, possibly to scare away would-be predators, or maybe just because they're another amazing example of God's "awe" factor in His creations placed there for us to enjoy!

God's acrobats

Prong & groove

Eyed elater

There are certain species in tropical countries (and South Florida) that are brilliantly bioluminescent like fireflies, only their glow comes from their thorax.

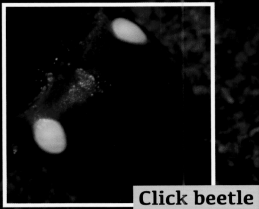

Click beetle
showing bioluminescence in Venezuela, South America

Click beetles will play dead for hours to avoid being eaten!

creepy cool!

Bug or insect? The true bugs belong to the order *Hemiptera* ['half wing'] and are known for their incomplete life cycle and sucking mouthparts. Examples of true bugs are the stink bug, the milkweed bug, and the giant water bug. Many are considered pests that eat our crops, like aphids, or attack us and carry diseases, like the infamous bed bug. Roaches are not in the same order as the true bugs, and although they are despised as carriers of disease, most species are important scavengers and decomposers. Believe it or not, some are even kept as pets!

Cockroach Structure

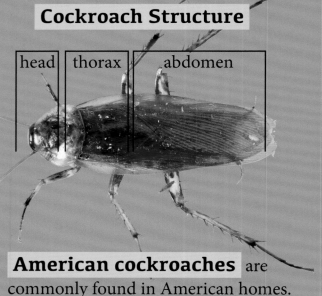

head | thorax | abdomen

American cockroaches are commonly found in American homes.

The **Headlight cockroach** (*Lucihormetica subcincta*) has yellow dots that actually glow! Found in Colombia, South America, these guys only glow in the wild and lose it when in captivity.

All insects have three body parts: a head, a thorax, and an abdomen.

creepy cool!

Found in tropical and subtropical climates, roaches can have an array of colors!

Giant rhinoceros burrowing roach, the largest species of roach, is found in Northern Australian tropical forests. Like the Madagascar hissing roach, they do not carry disease!

Devil's flower mantis

(*Idolomantis diabolica*) is one of the largest mantises on earth and is found in tropical East Africa.

The mantis is one of the few insects that can move its head 180 degrees!

creepy cool!

BUGS IN CAMO!

God has given many insects some of the most incredible camouflage in the animal kingdom. Like a soldier or a hunter who blends into his surroundings to hide from view, He has designed some insects in ways that appear to disguise them from predators and prey. With a mind blowing array of colors and patterns, some of these insects appear to be part plant! Let's take a look at a few of these masters of disguise!

Malaysian dead leaf mantis

(*Deroplatys lobata*)

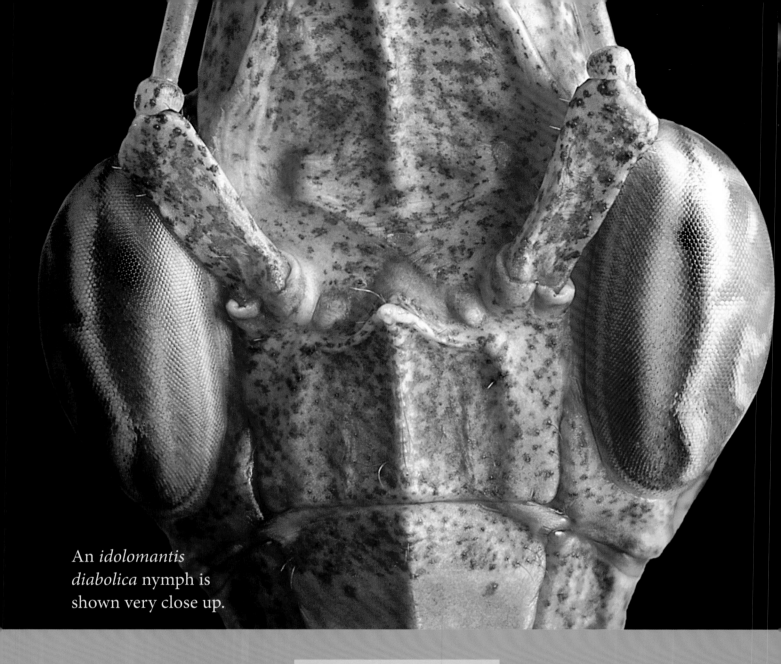

An *idolomantis diabolica* nymph is shown very close up.

The praying mantis

African ghost mantis
(Phyllocrania paradoxa)

One of the most incredible insects is the familiar praying mantis. These amazing insects are very alert and active, always ready to snatch a fly or bug with their well-designed front legs. Their legs have special claws that grasp their prey in a vice-like grip and are held in the typical "praying" fashion while they wait for their unsuspecting dinner. These insects are considered beneficial because they eat so many nuisance bugs like flies. They are designed to be perfectly camouflaged to blend in with their surroundings and even move like a swaying leaf in the wind. The people of China kept them as pets hundreds of years ago!

Devil's flower mantis
Idolomantis in threat pose

Malaysian dead leaf mantis
(Deroplatys lobata)

The orchid mantis
from Indonesia
(*Hymenopus coronatus*
and other species)

(Luc Viatour / www.Lucnix.be)

The amazing pink orchid mantis is something that takes your breath away! This could only come from the mind of our amazing Creator!

The beautiful colors of the orchid Mantis fade after it dies.

creepy cool!

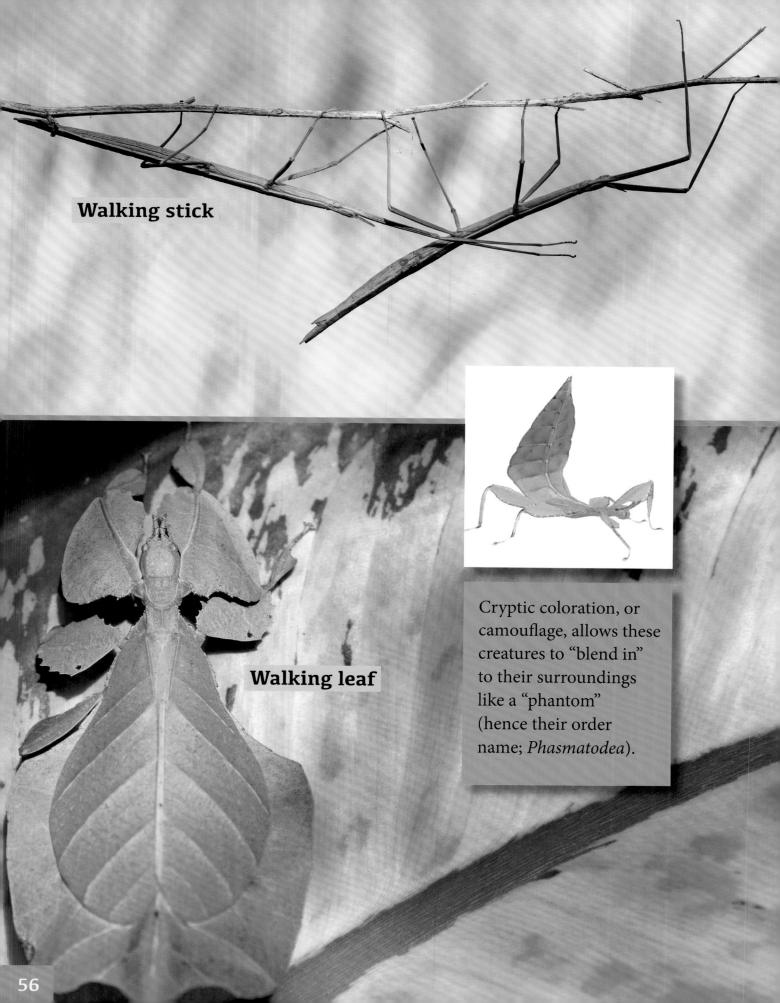

Walking stick

Walking leaf

Cryptic coloration, or camouflage, allows these creatures to "blend in" to their surroundings like a "phantom" (hence their order name; *Phasmatodea*).

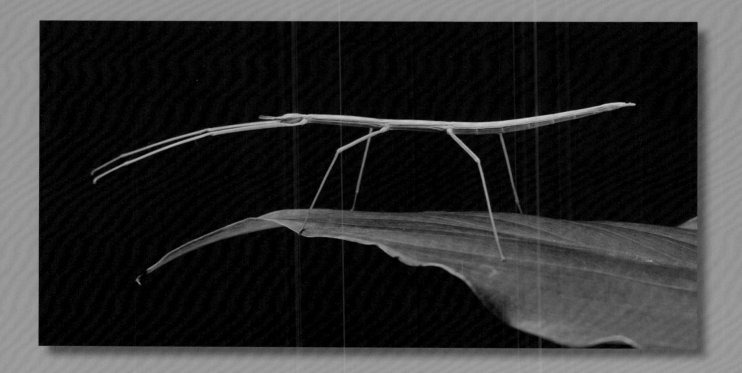

Australian walking stick

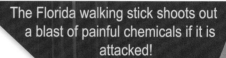

The Florida walking stick shoots out a blast of painful chemicals if it is attacked!

creepy cool!

Notice the "walking stick" and "walking leaf" and how closely they resemble their background habitat. Their heads resemble emerging buds, and they even move in a slow, rocking motion that looks like a branch or leaf swaying in a gentle breeze!

Antonio Pigafetta, who traveled with Magellan in the 1500s, thought walking leaves were real leaves that could walk!

creepy cool!

Leaf mantis from Peru

Imagine taking a leisurely stroll in an Indonesian rainforest, admiring the lush foliage, when all of the sudden, "Yikes!!! Did that leaf just get up and walk?" Their name, **"walking leaves"** (*Phyllidae*) wonderfully describes these living examples of God's creativity. Closely observe the intricate patterns that perfectly mimic the veins of a leaf, even with spots of discoloration that real leaves often have! Their colors vary from vivid greens, to bright yellows, to mottled browns. More rare are the oranges and reds, representing a full spectrum of leaf coloration! Some species even have "bite-mark patterns" on the edges of their bodies. The disguise is so complete, their own species have been observed taking a nibble out of each other!

The "false" leaf katydid is perfectly dressed for hiding as it lives and hunts in trees and shrubs. Often called a "leaf grasshopper," it is not really a grasshopper. Some grasshoppers are called "dead leaf grasshoppers" because they also camouflage themselves so well, even down to false "holes" on their body. By "mimicking" the appearance of leaves, they can protect themselves from creatures like birds and spiders that might want to eat them.

What is the difference between a katydid and a grasshopper? Both are from the scientific order or group called *Orthoptera*, or straight wings. Insects in this group may make sounds differently, but many of them have an "ear," called a tympanum, just below the knee on their front legs to hear sounds. Grasshoppers usually have ears on either side of their abdomens. Katydids are similar to crickets in that they make noise by rubbing their wings together. Grasshoppers make noise by rubbing their legs against their abdomen, not by rubbing their legs together.

False Leaf Katydid

The differences between katydids and grasshoppers:

- Grasshoppers usually eat only grasses or plants

- Katydids will eat plants, nectar, pollen, or other insects

- Grasshoppers and locusts usually have short antennae

- Usually long antennae for crickets and katydids

- Grasshoppers and locusts are usually active in the daytime

- Crickets and katydids are nocturnal, or active at night

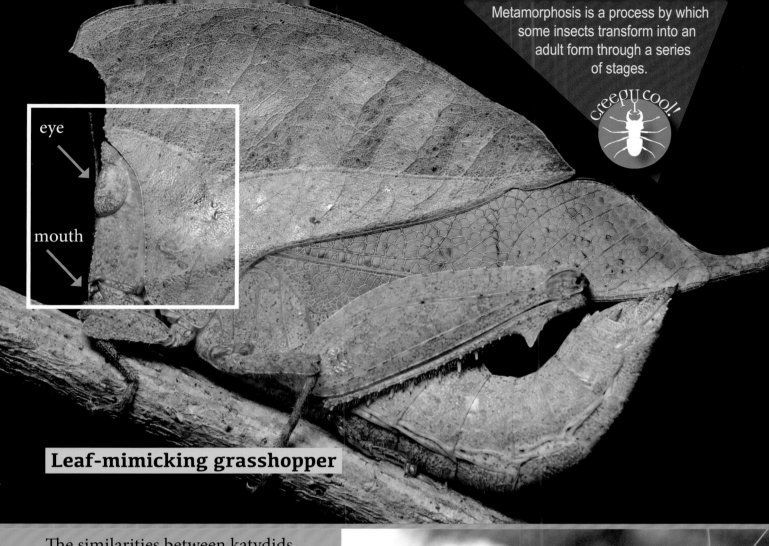

Metamorphosis is a process by which some insects transform into an adult form through a series of stages.

creepy cool!

eye

mouth

Leaf-mimicking grasshopper

The similarities between katydids and grasshoppers:

- Parts of mouth made for chewing

- Can make sounds

- Strong back legs for jumping

- Antennae (long, short, or thin)

Like all animals in our fallen world, insects get mutations and abnormalities such as albinism (no pigment/color) melanism (extra pigment/ dark color), and a very rare condition called erythrism (extra red or pink pigmentation). This makes for uniquely beautiful-colored **Pink katydids** currently being researched at the Audubon Nature Institute in New Orleans! Unfortunately, they are also easy targets for predators.

61

BIZARRE and BEAUTIFUL

Insects have even been the object of worship for some cultures. The most famous of these would be the ancient Egyptians, who revered the scarab, the dung beetle, which they thought represented their sun god rolling the sun across the sky. Some of the insects that follow are quite odd, and some have amazing beauty. You decide!

Jewel beetles have an amazing technicolor exoskeleton! (The genuses *Chrysina*, *Buprestidae*, and certain weevils, *Eupholus* and *Entimus*).

What advantage is a bright gold nugget?! The gold beetle actually reflects light at the same wavelength as the mineral! Probably the best explanation is that God made them for us to enjoy! That statement may offend those who view people as nothing more than evolved animals, but we know that our Creator made plants not only good for food, but also *"pleasant to the sight"* (Genesis 2:9). This principle applies to all of His creation!

Gold jewel beetle

Chrysina beetle

Some of the most eye-catching beetles look as if they were dipped in molten metal or hand painted with the most reflective colors imaginable! These "jewel scarabs," *Chrysina,* were actually used as jewelry by the local peoples of Central and South America. The vivid greens employed by the majority of the *Chrysina* species do conceal them well as they hide under leaves until night falls when most are active. The bright silver species act as a mirror that reflects their green surroundings well.

Jewel beetle
(Chrysina limbata)

Jewel beetle
(*Anthaxia fulgurans*)

In the past, and even today, people have used many of the patterns found on insects in their artwork, or even as decorative jewelry! The vivid and jewel-like appearance of many of these beetles has drawn people to make necklaces or other adornments for thousands of years. The beautiful colors are a combination of pigments and structural design that only reflects certain light. For example, the metallic appearance of the gold and silver jewel beetle is constructed in such a perfect way to refract only those colors. Only an all-wise and wonderful Creator could design such beauty!

A recent discovery that points again to our Creator is found in the incredible reflective properties of the beetle's exoskeleton. The "structural" design of the beetle's shell reflects different colors and gives the beetle that amazing metallic shine. There is a layer of uric acid under the outer layer of chitin or shell that allows this to happen. The beetle's shine also involves circular polarized light and exact mathematical properties, which can get very technical as the structures have to be so precise. The closer we look, the more amazing design features we see! Who knows what more will be discovered in the near future?

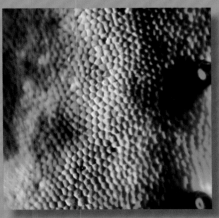

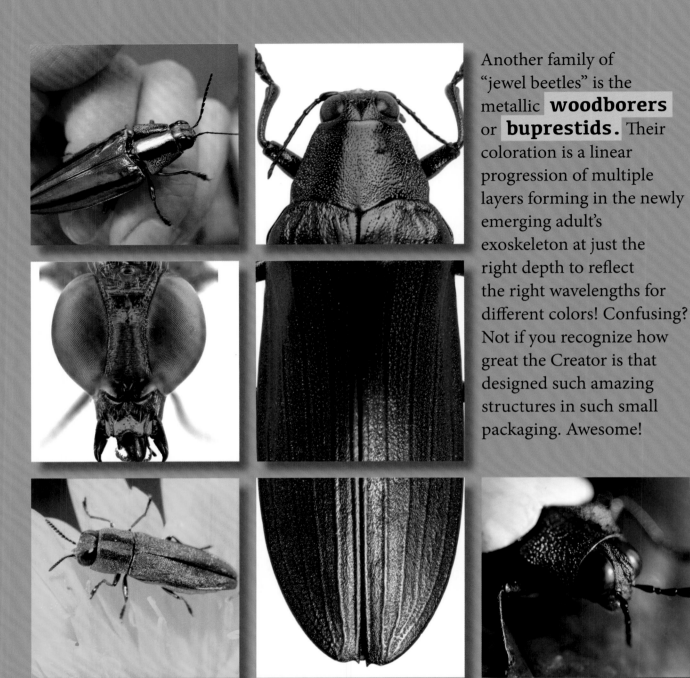

Another family of "jewel beetles" is the metallic **woodborers** or **buprestids.** Their coloration is a linear progression of multiple layers forming in the newly emerging adult's exoskeleton at just the right depth to reflect the right wavelengths for different colors! Confusing? Not if you recognize how great the Creator is that designed such amazing structures in such small packaging. Awesome!

Diamond weevils in the genus *Entimus* are another iridescent masterpiece of engineering. They have recently been discovered to possess a three-dimensional photonic crystal very similar to the structure of a diamond with its light-refracting abilities! These crystals are found on small scales within small pits across the beetle's body.

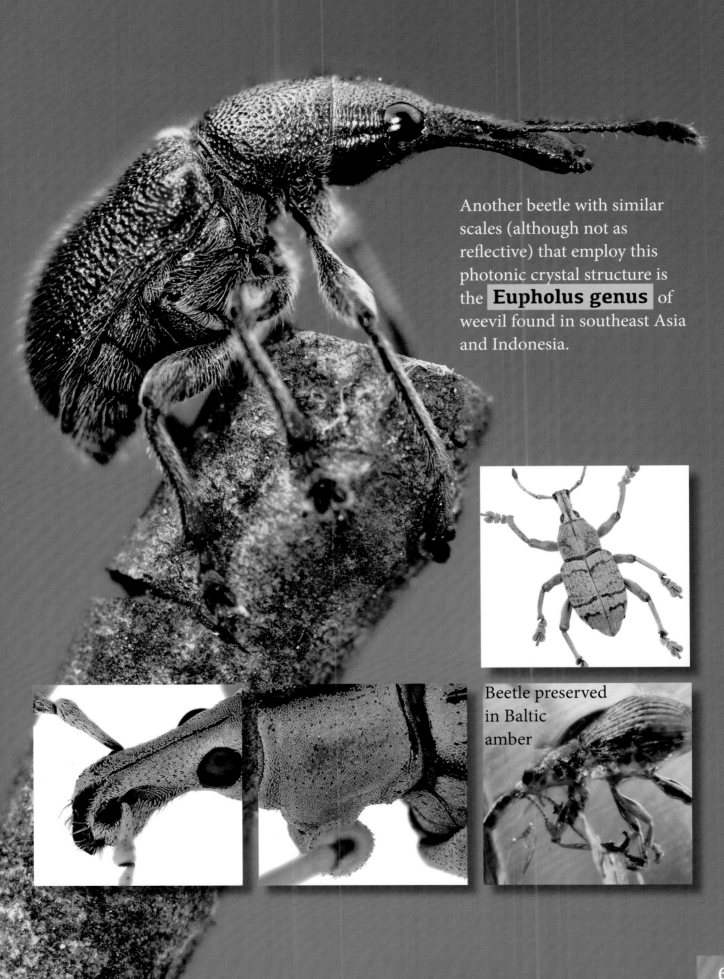

Another beetle with similar scales (although not as reflective) that employ this photonic crystal structure is the **Eupholus genus** of weevil found in southeast Asia and Indonesia.

Beetle preserved in Baltic amber

Leafhoppers release a liquid called honey-dew that ants and some other insects find sweet to eat!

creepy cool!

As we investigate and observe the creation around us, the more wonders we discover! Take, for example, a common **little leafhopper** (*Issus coleoptratus*) found in England. It actually possesses perfect little gears that help it jump straight! These gears are found in the back legs of nymphs. They work in tandem to keep the young bugs from veering off course due to "yaw." Again, we see precise measurements and impeccable design features found in some of the smallest creatures!

Furry beetles, otherwise known as metallic woodborers, are wonderful decomposers of wood and trees. Some African species have tufts of "hair" which make them appear furry! Others in this same family include the "jewel beetles." Jesus said in Matthew chapter 6:28-30: *"So why do you worry about clothing? Consider the lilies of the field, how they grow: they neither toil nor spin; and yet I say to you that even Solomon in all his glory was not arrayed like one of these. Now if God so clothes the grass of the field, which today is, and tomorrow is thrown into the oven, will He not much more clothe you, O you of little faith?"* Just think about these beautiful little creatures that God has made, and how much more He cares for you!

The **Scorpion beetle** *(Onychocerus albitarsis)* is a small beetle from South America, only recently discovered, it has an actual stinger at the end of each antennae! Collectors were noticing slight discomfort and swelling after handling this species, and thus discovered the stinging longhorn beetle! Currently, this is the only beetle known to possess a venomous sting. After electron microscopes carefully examined this guy, many people said how closely the stingers resemble scorpion stingers.

The **Cyphochilus beetle** of southeast Asia may be one of the "whitest whites" in nature, and scientists are studying how to copy the design feature of this beetle. White this bright is rare in creation, and it demands a specific kind of scattering of light. This is done by specially designed flat scales. They are currently being used to develop extremely bright but lightweight paper!

Papilio ulysses

Butterflies actually taste with their feet!

creepy cool!

The blackest black can be found on the wings of the Indonesian male **birdwing butterfly** (*Ornithoptera priamus*) and *Papilio ulysses*, the "Mountain Blue" from Indonesia and Australia. The dark black coloration comes not only from pigments in the scales but also from the "pitted" design feature that "soaks up," or traps, more surrounding light wavelengths. Amazing! Another example of the Master Artist!

What are the difference between butterflies and moths? While there are always exceptions in the insect world, in general the differences are as follows:

1. Antennae: Moths have feathery ones, while butterflies' are thin with a small club at the end.

2. Active: Most moths are active at night, while butterflies are active during the day.

3. Resting: Moths rest with their wings spread to the side or close to their backs; butterflies rest with wings above their back.

4. Color of wings: Butterflies are usually more brightly colored, while moths are usually brown, gray, or black.

5. Pupae (their state before changing): Moths emerge from a silk cocoon while butterflies emerge from a hard-shelled chrysalis.

Morpho wing scales are transparent! The intense blue color comes from precisely designed structures that only refract the blue wavelength!

creepy cool!

Helicopter damselfly
(*Microstigma rotundatum*)

The Helicopter damselfly is one of the largest damselflies on Earth! With a wingspan reaching up to 7½ inches (19 cm) in the large males, it is considered the largest of the order *Odonata* (which also includes the dragonfly). Found in tropical Central and South America (with a similar species in tropical Africa), they fly with a slow, deliberate up-and-down style in the thick understory of tropical rainforests. Those who have seen them flying through the deep, dark jungle say they have a "ghost-like" appearance, with their white wing patches and large size. They need to fly slowly when searching for their favorite food — spiders!

Hovering in front of a prospective meal, the helicopter damselfly will dart in and grab the unsuspecting spider right out of the center of its web, and then munch down after removing the spider's legs. It has to be quick and accurate, otherwise the hunter may become the hunted! Another curious feature about these damselflies is that they only lay their eggs in pockets of trapped rainwater found in the nooks and holes in trunks of giant trees or in large plants called bromeliads. Unfortunately, due to their size, appetite, and limited growing space, usually only one niad (baby damselfly) emerges as an adult, after it has eaten its own brothers and sisters! The niads also consume multitudes of mosquito larvae, and therefore should be considered a beneficial insect with conservation in mind and protection of the large old-forest growth trees in which they dwell.

This dragonfly fossil from Germany reveals how the Flood of Noah created massive fossils from all the water and soil that was stirred up.

77

Ants
Proverbs 6:6-8

Bees
Psalm 118:12

Beetles
Leviticus 11:20-23

Caterpillar
Psalm 78:46

Consider all the incredible bugs in this book, with their incredible design features and variations! If God cares enough to create these marvelous works of art, and give them each a purpose in life, just imagine how much more He cares for you!

Gnats
Matthew 23:24

Grasshoppers
Leviticus 11:22

Enjoy these brilliant signposts of God's grand design as you observe the amazing photos and remember that the great Creator who has made these awesome insects cares much more about YOU! He has a plan for YOUR life and loves you more than words can say!

Hornets
Exodus 23:28

Locust
Proverbs 30:27

Flies
Exodus 8:21

Moth
Matthew 6:19

words to know

Abdomen—Sometimes called the belly or stomach, it is the last part of a bug, after the head and thorax.

Antennae—This pair of "feelers" on the head of bugs helps them feel the world, and sometimes taste and smell it, too.

Bioluminescence—Used by fireflies and other bugs, this light is created by chemicals mixing with oxygen.

Bugs—True bugs belong to the order Hemiptera (half wing) and are known for their incomplete life cycle and sucking mouthparts.

Camouflage—Different bugs were designed by God with camouflage, blending in with their surroundings to protect themselves from creatures that want to eat them.

Carnivores—These are creatures that only eat meat, and are not vegetarians, which only eat plants, or omnivores, which eat meat and plants.

Decaying—Decay is the breaking down of once-living materials, like dead plants in a forest, this decay creates a banquet for certain types of bugs.

Decomposers—These are bugs that help once-living materials decompose or break down in ways that help feed the soil and make it healthier.

Dissect—When a scientist dissects something, he or she takes it apart to examine how it functions, including what it eats and how it breathes.

Ecosystem—This is an area of the world where specific living things are made for the nonliving world around them, forming a unique place like a pond or mountain region.

Elytra—The elytra are the hardened portions of a bug meant to protect their wings underneath. Some bugs cannot fly because their elytra are stuck together.

Entomology—This is the study of insects, and refers to the segments or parts of the insect/bug that it is divided into.

Entomophagy—A big word given for people who eat insects for food, from Australia to Africa to Asia to the United States.

Evolution—The false belief that all life came from nothing, by sheer accident, and not by God's powerful hand as the Bible so clearly declares.

Exoskeleton—The outer shell of a bug, its skeleton, which helps protect it from predators and helps it hold water.

Grubs—The larvae or young of an insect, which many people around the world eat for protein.

Insect—This is a class of creature that has an exoskeleton, three pairs of legs, one set of antennae, and three body parts (head, thorax, and abdomen).

Iridescent—Iridescence refers to the brilliant, beautiful colors displayed on an object, with many bugs covered in rainbow-like jewels.

Larvae—The young of an insect, which often transform into adults through some massive change or metamorphosis.

Larvae stage—During the larvae stage, the young bugs often have huge appetites, which helps them have the energy they need to transform into their adult form.

Ligaments—These are thick muscle strands that connect a bug's legs to its hard exoskeleton.

Luciferin/Luciferase—Fireflies use the substances luciferin and luciferase in combination with oxygen, magnesium, and ATP (adenosine triphosphate) to produce cold light.

Mandibles—These are the jaws of a bug that can help it bite prey, carry objects, or defend itself against certain enemies.

Metamorphosis—This is the process by which some insects transform into an adult form through a series of stages.

Mimic—To mimic means to copy or imitate something else, which some bugs have been designed by God to do, like leaf and stick bugs.

Parasites—A parasite is a creature or organism that feeds on another organism, called a host, bringing sickness or eventual death to the host.

Pigments—These are hues or tones of color that create such beautiful displays on certain bugs, or that create colors that help camouflage other bugs.

Pollinators—Insects and other creatures are pollinators when they help transfer pollen or seeds from one flower to another to help fertilize them to produce more.

Predators—These are creatures that hunt and kill other creatures for food.

Pupa stage—Some bugs have several growth stages, and the pupa stage comes after the larval stage and before the adult stage.

Scavengers—These are creatures that seek out food sources from the waste or garbage others leave behind.

Setae—Specially designed bristle-like hairs on some bugs that can help them move or assist them to trap air, if under water.

Thorax—The middle portion of an insect between the head and the abdomen.

Toxin—A substance that is poisonous or harmful if touched or swallowed.

Tympanum—This is an "ear" just below the knee on the front legs of certain insects.

Hercules beetle

Large toothed longhorn beetle

Namib desert beetle

Whirligig beetle

Diving beetle

Giraffe weevil

Common name	Namib desert beetle (Fog basking beetle)
Scientific name	*Stenocara*
Length	About 1 in 2.5 cm
Lifespan	About 1 year
Location	Namibia, South West Africa
Diet	Decaying plants

The Creator has given these beetles a very bumpy shell on their backs, which was shown to attract and collect water directly from the air!

Common name	Large-toothed longhorn beetle
Scientific name	*Macrodontia cervicornis*
Length	3–6.75 in 7.5–17 cm
Lifespan	Over 10 years! (Most as a larvae; only a few months as adult.)
Location	Rainforests of South America
Diet	Larva eat rotting wood; adults eat tree sap

The larvae of this beetle feed on decaying wood and have been considered a delicacy for hundreds of years!

Common name	Hercules beetle
Scientific name	*Dynastes hercules*
Length	2–6.75 in 5–17 cm
Lifespan	3 years (most of that spent as a larvae)
Location	Rainforests of South & Central America and Lesser Antilles
Diet	Larva eat rotting wood; adults eat fruit

One of the world's largest beetles, with lengths up to seven inches (over 17 cm), these living tanks are also considered the strongest creatures for their size!

Common name	Giraffe weevils
Scientific name	*Trachelophorus giraffe*
Length	About 1 in 2.5 cm
Lifespan	A few days up to a year
Location	Madagascar
Diet	Leaves of the giraffe beetle tree

The enlarged head of this bug extends over half the length of its body!

Common name	Diving beetles
Scientific name	*Dytiscidae*
Length	1–2 in 2.5 –5 cm
Lifespan	1–3 years
Location	Worldwide
Diet	Carnivore and scavenger (even eating small fish and frogs)

They can submerge themselves for at least ten minutes by utilizing their specially designed wing covers and hairs on their abdomen to trap a bubble of air!

Common name	Whirligig beetles
Scientific name	*Grinidae*
Length	About 1 in .5–3.5 cm
Lifespan	About 1 year
Location	Worldwide
Diet	Carnivore and scavenger

The amazing whirligig beetle has two divided eyes, and these "four" eyes can see above and below the water at the same time!

Firefly

Mantis

Walking leaf

Birdwing butterfly

Leafhopper

Damselflies

Common name	Walking leaves
Scientific name	*Phyllidae*
Length	2–5 in 5–13 cm
Lifespan	About 1 year
Location	Southeast Asia to Australia
Diet	Leaves

Some species have "bite-mark patterns" on their bodies, and this disguise is so complete, their own species have been observed taking a nibble from each other!

Common name	Mantis
Scientific name	*Mantodea*
Length	1 to almost 6 in 2.5–14 cm
Lifespan	About 1 year
Location	Worldwide
Diet	Carnivore

Mantis legs have special claws which grasp their prey in a vice-like grip and are held in the typical "praying" fashion while they wait for dinner!

Common name	Fireflies (Lightning bugs)
Scientific name	*Lampridae*
Length	About 1 in 2.5 cm
Lifespan	About 1 year, mostly as a larva and only a week or two as an adult
Location	Worldwide
Diet	Larva eat snails, slugs, and worms; adults may feed on nectar (some eat other fireflies)

Fireflies use a complex arrangement of chemicals to produce bright, visible light called "bioluminescence."

Common name	Helicopter damselflies
Scientific name	*Pseudostigmatidae*
Length	Up to 7.5 in 19 cm
Lifespan	Up to two years
Location	Tropical South America and Africa
Diet	Spiders

With a wingspan reaching up to 7½ inches (19 cm), it is considered the largest of the order *Odonata* (which also includes the dragonflies)!

Common name	Leafhopper
Scientific name	*Issue coleoptratus*
Length	About 0.5 in 1.2 cm
Lifespan	About 1 month
Location	Europe, but leafhoppers are worldwide
Diet	Plant juices, sap

They actually possess perfect little gears that help them jump straight!

Common name	Birdwing butterfly
Scientific name	*Ornithoptera priamus*
Length	The largest (*O. alexandrae*) up to 12 in (30 cm)
Lifespan	About 7 months
Location	Indonesia, New Guinea, and North Australia
Diet	Caterpillars feed on Aristolochia, a rare poisonous vine; adults feed on flower nectar

The black coloration comes from pigments in the scales and from the "pitted" design feature that "soaks up," or traps more surrounding light wavelengths!